the practice of the presence OF GOD

by brother Lawrence

the practice of the presence OF GOD

by brother Lawrence

WHITAKER HOUSE

Editor's note: This book has been edited for the modern reader. Words, expressions, and sentence structure have been updated for clarity and readability.

THE PRACTICE OF THE PRESENCE OF GOD

ISBN: 0-88368-105-6
Printed in the United States of America
© 1982 by Whitaker House
Cover photo © by Russ Lamb/H. Armstrong Roberts

Whitaker House
30 Hunt Valley Circle
New Kensington, PA 15068

22 23 24 25 26 27 28 29 / 10 09 08 07 06 05 04 03 02

Contents

Part Three: Spiritual Maxims

Part Four: The Life of Brother Lawrence

Preface

The Practice of the Presence of God is a collection of Brother Lawrence's spiritual insights into the heart of God, as revealed through his letters, conversations, and his life itself. Written over three hundred years ago, this message is relevant for every Christian who is caught up in the rush of today's world.

Each section, whether written by the author's own hand or by his close friend, Joseph de Beaufort, reveals the inner secrets of Brother Lawrence's heart—a heart that had learned the most essential ingredient of the Christian life: how to remain in the presence of God.

In this abridged edition, we have sought to update and clarify the language of this Christian classic, paraphrasing where necessary, while keeping the essence of the message intact.

We trust that Brother Lawrence's lifelong endeavor to dwell completely in the presence of God will become a continual practice for all who read this book.

— *The Publisher*

Part One

❖ ◈ ❖

Conversations

First Conversation

I met Brother Lawrence for the first time today. He told me that God had been especially good to him in his conversion. He was eighteen at the time and still in the world. He told me that it had all happened one winter day, as he was looking at a barren tree. Although the tree's leaves were indeed gone, he knew that they would soon reappear, followed by blossoms and then fruit. This gave him a profound impression of God's providence and power, which never left him. Brother Lawrence still maintains that this impression detached him entirely from the world and gave him such a great love for God that it hasn't changed in all of the forty years he has been walking with Him.

Brother Lawrence had formerly been a servant to the treasurer of the monastery and had been very clumsy. He believed that in order to be saved, he would have to be punished for this clumsiness. Thus, he sacrificed all of the pleasures in his life to God. However, rather than punishing him, God gave him nothing but wholehearted satisfaction. He would tell the

11

Lord endearingly and often that he felt deceived, because his Christian walk had thus far been so pleasant and not filled with suffering as he had anticipated.

Brother Lawrence insisted that, to be constantly aware of God's presence, it is necessary to form the habit of continually talking with Him throughout each day. To think that we must abandon conversation with Him in order to deal with the world is erroneous. Instead, as we nourish our souls by seeing God in His exaltation, we will derive a great joy at being His.

Another thing he mentioned was that our faith is too weak. Instead of letting faith rule our lives, we are guided by our petty, everyday, mechanical prayers, which are always changing. The church's only road to the perfection of Christ is faith.

The dear brother remarked that we must give ourselves totally to God in both temporal and spiritual affairs. Our only happiness should come from doing God's will, whether it brings us some pain or great pleasure. After all, if we are truly devoted to doing God's will, pain and pleasure won't make any difference to us.

We also need to be faithful, even in dry periods. It is during those dry spells that God tests our love for Him. We should take advantage of those times to practice our determination and

our surrender to Him. This will often bring us to
a maturity further on in our walk with God.

Brother Lawrence wasn't surprised by the
amount of sin and unhappiness in the world.
Rather, he wondered why there wasn't more,
considering the extremes to which the enemy is
capable of going. He said he prayed about it, but
because he knew God could rectify the situation
in a moment if He willed it, he didn't allow himself to become greatly concerned.

To succeed in giving ourselves to God as
much as He desires, we must constantly guard
our souls. In addition to being involved in spiritual matters, the soul is involved in the things of
this world. However, when we turn our backs on
Him, exposing our souls to the world, He will not
so easily answer our call. When we are willing to
accept God's help and guard our souls according
to His desires, we may commune with Him
whenever we like.

Second Conversation

*B*rother Lawrence said that he was always guided by love. He was never influenced by any other interest, including whether or not he was saved. He was content doing the smallest chore if he could do it purely for the love of God. He even found himself quite well off, which he attributed to the fact that he sought only God and not His gifts. He believed that God is much greater than any of the simple gifts He gives us. Rather than desiring them from Him, he chose to look beyond the gifts, hoping to learn more about God Himself. Sometimes he even wished that he could avoid receiving his reward so that he would have the pleasure of doing something solely for God.

For some years, Brother Lawrence had been quite disturbed because he wasn't certain that he was saved. Even so, he maintained the attitude that he had become a Christian because he loved the Lord, and so he would continue to love Him, whether he was certain of his salvation or not. That way, he would at least have the earthly pleasure of doing everything he could for the love of God. (Later, this uncertainty about his relationship with God left Brother Lawrence.)

After that, he did not dwell on thoughts of heaven or hell. His life was filled with freedom and rejoicing. Lifting all his sins up to God, he tried to show Him how undeserving of His grace he was, but the Lord continued to bless him. Sometimes God even took our brother by the hand and led him before the heavenly court, to show off His lowly servant whom He was pleased to honor.

In the beginning, Brother Lawrence declared that a little effort was needed to form the habit of continuously conversing with God, telling Him everything that was happening. However, after a little careful practice, God's love refreshed him, and it all became quite easy.

Whenever he considered doing some good deed, he always consulted God about it, saying, "Lord, I will never be able to do that if You don't help me." Immediately he would be given more than enough strength.

When he sinned, he confessed it to God with these words: "I can do nothing better without You. Please keep me from falling and correct the mistakes I make." After that, he did not feel guilty about the sin.

Brother Lawrence pointed out that he spoke very simply and frankly to God. He asked for help with things as he needed it, and his experience had been that God never failed to respond.

Only recently, Brother Lawrence was asked to go into Burgundy to get supplies for the monastery. This chore was difficult for him because, first, he had no head for business and, second, he was lame in one leg and could not walk on the boat without falling against the cargo of barrels. Nevertheless, neither his awkwardness nor the errand in general caused him any distress. He simply told God that it was His affair, after which he found that everything turned out nicely.

Things went the same way in the kitchen of the monastery, where he worked. Although he once had a great dislike for kitchen work, he developed quite a facility for doing it over the fifteen years he was there. He attributed this to his doing everything for the love of God, asking as often as possible for grace to do his work. He said that he was presently in the shoe repair shop and that he liked it very much. He would, however, be willing to work anywhere, always rejoicing at being able to do little things for the love of God.

Brother Lawrence was aware of his sins and was not at all surprised by them. "That is my nature," he would say, "the only thing I know how to do." He simply confessed his sins to

God, without pleading with Him or making ex-cuses. After this, he was able to peacefully re-sume his regular activity of love and adoration. If Brother Lawrence didn't sin, he thanked God for it, because only God's grace could keep him from sinning.

When he was troubled by something, he seldom consulted anyone about it. Knowing only that God was present, he walked in the light of faith and was content just to lose himself in God's love no matter what happened. There, in God's love, he would find himself again.

He remarked that thinking often spoils everything and that evil usually begins with our thoughts. In Brother Lawrence's opinion, we should reject any thoughts that distract us from serving the Lord or that undermine our salva-tion. Freeing the mind of such thoughts permits a comfortable conversation with God, but Brother Lawrence added that this isn't always easy. When he was first saved, he had often spent his entire prayer time rejecting distrac-tions and then falling immediately into them again.

He said that a sharp distinction should be drawn between acts of the intellect and those of the will. The former are of little importance, while the latter mean everything. All we really have to do is to love God and rejoice in Him.

He declared that all the possible good works or self-abasing acts of contrition we could possibly do would not erase a single sin. In fact, God often chooses those who had been the greatest sinners to receive His greatest grace, because this can reveal His goodness more dramatically.

Only the blood of Jesus Christ can cleanse us of sin. For this reason, we should strive to love Him with all our hearts.

Brother Lawrence said he concentrated on doing little things for Him, since he was unable to do bigger things. After that, anything the Lord willed could happen to him, and he wouldn't be concerned about it. Therefore, he didn't worry about anything and asked God for nothing except that he might not offend Him.

Third Conversation

*B*rother Lawrence confided to me that the foundation of his spiritual life was the faith that revealed to him the exalted position of God. Once this became secure in the depths of his heart, he was easily able to do all his actions for the love of God. He truly understood that this solid faith in God was a great honor to Him and gave the Lord an open door to answer his prayers and shower blessings upon him.

He continued that if someone surrenders himself entirely to God, resolving to do anything for Him, the Lord will protect that person from deception. He will also not allow such a person to suffer through trials for very long, but will give him a way of escape that he might endure it (1 Corinthians 10:13).

Brother Lawrence's heartfelt goal was to think of nothing but God. If he did allow some time to pass without thinking of Him, he did not grow upset about it. Once he confessed his weakness to God, he returned to Him with all the more confidence and joy because he had found himself so unhappy apart from God's presence. If he felt any ungracious thought or any temptation generating, he would not panic or feel helpless to resist it. This was because his past experience of God's faithful assistance allowed him to wait until just the right moment to call out. When the time came, he would address himself to God, and the evil thoughts would vanish right away.

Because of this same trust in God's care, when Brother Lawrence had some outside business to attend to, he never worried about it beforehand. Rather, he found God would give him a picture as clear as a mirror image of exactly what to do at precisely the right moment. He had acted in this way for quite some time, without being concerned about something ahead of time. Before he had experienced God's swift help in his affairs, he had attempted to plan every detail, doing the job in his own strength. Now, though, acting with childlike simplicity in God's sight, he did everything for the love of God, thanking Him for His guidance. Everything he did passed calmly, in a way that held him close to the loving presence of God.

When any outside business unnecessarily diverted him from his communication with God, a little reminder came from the Lord that took possession of his soul, flooding it with the image of God. This sometimes set him on fire to the point that he felt a great impulse to shout praises, to sing, and to dance before the Lord with joy.

Brother Lawrence declared that he felt much closer to God in his day-to-day activities than most people ever believed to be possible.

The worst trial he could imagine was losing his sense of God's presence, which had been with him for so long a time. However, his confidence in God's goodness made him certain that He would never leave him entirely. Should he encounter any great difficulty in his life, he knew the Lord would provide the strength he needed to endure it.

With this assurance, Brother Lawrence wasn't afraid of anything. He added that he wasn't afraid of dying to self or losing himself in Christ, because complete surrender to God's will is the only secure road to follow. In it, there is always enough light to assure safe travel.

In the beginning, it is always necessary to be faithful, both in actions and in the renouncing of self. After that, there is only indescribable joy. If difficulties arise, simply turn to Jesus Christ and pray for His grace, with which everything will become easy.

Our brother remarked that some people go only as far as their regular devotions, stopping there and neglecting love, which is the purpose of those devotions. This could easily be seen in their actions and explained why they possessed so little solid virtue.

Neither skill nor knowledge is needed to go to God, he added. All that is necessary is a heart dedicated entirely and solely to Him out of love for Him above all others.

Fourth Conversation

*T*oday Brother Lawrence spoke to me quite openly and with great enthusiasm about his manner of going to God. He said the most important part resides in renouncing, once and for all, whatever does not lead to God. This allows us to become involved in a continuous conversation with Him in a simple and unhindered manner.

All we have to do is to recognize God as being intimately present within us. Then we may speak directly to Him every time we need to ask for help, to know His will in moments of uncertainty, and to do whatever He wants us to do in a way that pleases Him. We should offer our work to Him before we begin and thank Him afterward for the privilege of having done it for His sake. This continuous conversation should also include praising and loving God incessantly for His infinite goodness and perfection.

Brother Lawrence declared that we ought to ask confidently for God's grace in everything we do, trusting the infinite merits of our Lord rather than our own thoughts. He said that God would never fail to give us His grace, and that he could testify to this personally. This brother in the Lord sinned only when he strayed from God's company or when he forgot to ask Him for His help.

When we are in doubt, he continued, God never fails to show us the right way to go, as long as our only goal is to please Him and show our love for Him.

He thought it was a shame that some people pursued certain activities (which, he noted, they did rather imperfectly due to human shortcomings), mistaking the means for the end. He said that our sanctification does not depend as much on changing our activities as it does on doing them for God rather than for ourselves.

The most effective way Brother Lawrence had for communicating with God was to simply do his ordinary work. He did this obediently, out of a pure love of God, purifying it as much as was humanly possible. He believed it was a serious mistake to think of our prayer time as being different from any other. Our actions should unite us with God when we are involved in our daily activities, just as our prayers unite us with Him in our quiet devotions.

He said his prayers consisted totally and simply of God's presence. His soul was resting in God, having lost its awareness of everything but love of Him. When he wasn't in prayer, he felt practically the same way. Remaining near to God, he praised and blessed Him with all his strength. Because of this, his life was full of continual joy.

We must, Brother Lawrence remarked, trust in God and surrender completely to Him. He will not deceive us. Never tire of doing even the smallest things for Him, because He isn't impressed so much with the dimensions of our work as with the love in which it is done. We should not be discouraged if we fail in the beginning. This practice will eventually cause our efforts to become a pleasurable habit that we can do without thinking.

He said that in order to be sure we are doing God's will, we should simply develop an attitude of faith, hope, and love. We need not be concerned about anything else. It simply is not important and should only be regarded as the means of getting to the final goal of being entirely lost in the love of God. We should desire to love Him as perfectly as we can, in this life as well as in eternity.

Many things are possible for the person who has hope. Even more is possible for the person who has faith. Still more is possible for the person who knows how to love. But everything is possible for the person who practices all three virtues.

Brother Lawrence added that when we begin our Christian walk, we must remember that we have been living in the world, subject to all sorts of miseries, accidents, and poor dispositions from within. The Lord will cleanse and humble us in order to make us more like Christ. As we go through this cleansing process, we will grow closer to God.

Therefore, we should rejoice in our difficulties, bearing them as long as the Lord wills, because only through such trials will our faith become purified, more precious than gold. (See 1 Peter 1:7; 4:19.)

Part Two

❖ ◆ ❖

Letters

First Letter

*D*ear friend,

I'd like to use this occasion to inform you of the thoughts of one of our brothers concerning the wonderful results and the continual help he receives from the presence of God. We could both profit from them. *[It is believed that Brother Lawrence was referring to himself in the following. His humility restrained him from saying so.]*

For more than forty years, this brother's principal endeavor has been to stay as close as possible to God, doing, saying, and thinking nothing that might displease Him. He has no reason for doing this, except to show his gratitude for God's pure love and because God deserves infinitely more than that anyway.

This brother has become so accustomed to God's divine presence that he relies on it for help on all sorts of occasions. His soul has been filled with a constant inner joy that is sometimes so overwhelming, he feels compelled to do what may seem to some as childish things, in order to prevent the feeling from becoming too intense.

If he sometimes strays from this divine presence, God immediately recalls him by communicating with him through the Holy Spirit. This often happens to him when he is busiest with his work. He responds faithfully to God's calling, either by offering his heart to God, by a tender, loving look, or by some affectionate words, such as, "My God, I am all Yours; do what You will with me." Then it is almost as if this God of love returns to his soul to rest again, satisfied with these few words. Experiencing these things makes this brother certain beyond all doubt that God is always in the depth of his soul, no matter what he does or what happens to him.

Imagine what contentment and satisfaction he enjoys, possessing such an ever-present treasure! He isn't anxious to find it and doesn't worry about where to look for it, because he has already found it and may take whatever he wants from it.

He often calls men blind, complaining that we are content with too little. God has infinite treasures to give us, he says. Why should we be satisfied with a brief moment of worship? With such meager devotion, we restrain the flow of God's abundant grace. If God can find a soul filled with a lively faith, He pours His grace into it in a torrent that, having found an open channel, gushes out exuberantly.

We often stop this torrent by our lack of respect for it. However, we mustn't restrain it any longer. Let us go into our hearts, dear friend, breaking down the dike, making way for grace, and making up for lost time! You and I are getting along in years. We may have little time left to live. Death is always near, so be prepared, for we only die once.

Once again, let us examine our inner selves. Time is pressing down on us, and each of us must be responsible for himself. I believe you have prepared yourself properly, so you won't be taken by surprise. I respect you for this; it is, after all, our business to be as open as possible to God's grace. However, we must continuously walk in God's Spirit, since in the spirit-life not to advance is to fall back.

Those who have the wind of the Holy Spirit in their souls glide ahead even while they sleep. If the vessel of our soul is still being tossed by winds or storms, we should wake the Lord who has been resting with us all along, and He will swiftly calm the sea.

I have taken the liberty, my dear friend, of telling you all this so you might reexamine your own relationship with God. If by some means (I pray it is not so) it has cooled even slightly, perhaps our brother's attitude will rekindle and inflame it. Do you remember our first enthusiasm and love for God? We could both recall it by way of this brother's example. He isn't well-known, in worldly terms, but with God he is tenderly loved and caressed. Let us pray earnestly for one another to receive this grace for ourselves.

Second Letter

M *y dear friend,*

Today I received two books and a letter from a mutual friend who is preparing to commit her whole life in service to the Lord. She has asked for both of our prayers as she makes her firm resolution to live her life for Him.

I am sending you one of the books, which discusses the importance of God's presence, so you know that it is close to my heart.

I still believe that all spiritual life consists of practicing God's presence and that anyone who practices it correctly will soon attain spiritual fulfillment.

To accomplish this, it is necessary for the heart to be emptied of everything that would offend God. He wants to possess our hearts completely. Before any work can be done in our souls, God must be totally in control.

There is no sweeter manner of living in the world than continuous communion with God. Only those who have experienced it can understand. However, I don't advise you to practice it for the sole purpose of gaining consolation for your problems. Seek it, rather, because God wills it and out of love for Him.

If I were a preacher, I would preach nothing but practicing the presence of God. If I were to be responsible for guiding souls in the right direction, I would urge everyone to be aware of God's constant presence, if for no other reason than because His presence is a delight to our souls and spirits.

It is, however, also necessary. If we only knew how much we need God's grace, we would never lose touch with Him. Believe me. Make a commitment never to deliberately stray from Him, to live the rest of your life in His holy presence. Don't do this in expectation of receiving heavenly comforts; simply do it out of love for Him.

Put your hand to the task! If you do it right, you will soon see the results. I will support you with my prayers. Please keep me in your prayers, also, and in the prayers of your church.

Third Letter

D *ear friend,*

I'm amazed that you haven't let me know your opinion of the book I sent you. You must have received it by now. Practice it energetically, even in your old age. It truly is better late than never.

I honestly cannot understand how people who claim to love the Lord can be content without practicing His presence. My preference is to retire with Him to the deepest part of my soul as often as possible. When I am with Him there, nothing frightens me, but the slightest diversion away from Him is painful to me.

Spending time in God's presence doesn't weaken the body. Leaving the seemingly innocent and permissible pleasures of the world for a time will, on the contrary, give us comfort. In fact, God won't allow a soul that is searching for Him to be comforted anywhere other than with Him. Hence, it makes sense to sacrifice ourselves for some time in His presence.

This does not mean that you have to suffer in this endeavor. No, God must be served with holy freedom. We should labor faithfully, without distress or anxiety, calmly recalling our spirit to God whenever it is distracted.

The only requirement is that we place our confidence entirely in God. Abandon any other concerns, including any special devotions you've undertaken simply as a means to an end. God is our "end." If we are diligently practicing His presence, we shouldn't need our former "means." We can continue our exchange of love with Him by just remaining in His holy presence. Adore Him and praise Him! There are so many ways we can thank Him. The Holy Spirit dwelling in us leads us to love God in a diversity of ways.

God be with all of you.

Fourth Letter

M y dear sister in the Lord,

I sympathize with your difficult situation. I think that freeing yourself of your present responsibilities for a while and devoting yourself entirely to prayer would be the best thing you could do for yourself. God does not ask much of you. But remembering Him, praising Him, asking for His grace, offering Him your troubles, or thanking Him for what He has given you will console you all the time. During your meals or during any daily duty, lift your heart up to Him, because even the least little remembrance will please Him. You don't have to pray out loud; He's nearer than you can imagine.

It isn't necessary that we stay in church in order to remain in God's presence. We can make our hearts personal chapels where we can enter anytime to talk to God privately. These conversations can be so loving and gentle, and anyone can have them.

Is there any reason not to begin? He may be waiting for us to take the first step. Because we have such a short time to live, we should spend our remaining time with God. Even suffering will be easier when we are with Him, but without Him, even the greatest pleasures will be joyless. May He be blessed in everything!

Gradually train yourself to show your love for Him by asking for His grace. Offer your heart to Him at every moment. Don't restrict your love of Him with rules or special devotions. Go out in faith, with love and humility.

I remain your servant in the Lord.

Fifth Letter

*D*ear Reverend,

I would like very much to know your opinion of my current situation. A few days ago, I was talking to a friend of mine about spiritual life. This friend described it as a life of grace, which begins with the fear and respect of a servant, growing through the hope of eternal life, finally to find fullness in pure love. She also said that different people experience this consummate love to greater and lesser degrees.

I haven't followed any particular steps in my own spiritual growth. On the contrary, I found methods to be discouraging. My intent, at the beginning of my Christian walk, was to give myself to God all at once. I did this out of love for Him, because I wanted to pay for my sins and renounce everything that offended Him.

My first prayers were about death, judgment, hell, heaven, and my sins. This went on for several years. When I wasn't praying, I kept myself carefully in God's presence, even while I was working. I knew He was always near me, in the deepest part of my heart. This gave me such great respect for God that I was content with faith alone. I continued to pray this way, which gave me enormous peace and Joy.

During the first ten years, however, I worried that my walk with the Lord wasn't good enough. Because I couldn't forget my past sins, I felt very guilty when I thought of all the grace He had shown me. During that time, I used to fall often and then get up again. It seemed that everything—even God—was against me and that only faith was on my side. Sometimes I believed I felt this way because I was trying to show, at the beginning of my walk, the same maturity it had taken other Christians years to achieve. Sometimes it got so bad that I thought I was on my way to hell—willfully offending God—and that there was no salvation for me.

Thankfully, these worries did not weaken my faith in God, but actually made it stronger. When I finally reached the point where I expected the rest of my life to be very difficult, I suddenly found myself wholly changed. My soul, which had always been troubled, finally came to rest in a profound inner peace.

Since that time, I have been serving God simply, in humility and faith. Out of love, I try not to say, do, or think anything that might offend Him. My only request is that He do whatever He pleases with me.

I feel unable to express what is going on inside me right now. I'm not anxious about my purpose in life because I only want to do God's will. I wouldn't even lift a straw from the ground against His order or for any other motive than love for Him. Pure love of Him is all that keeps me going.

I have given up all but my intercessory prayers to focus my attention on remaining in His holy presence. I keep my attention on God in a simple, loving way. This is my soul's secret experience of the actual, unceasing presence of God. It gives me such contentment and joy that I sometimes feel compelled to do rather childish things to control it.

To sum up, kind sir, I am sure my soul has been with God for more than thirty years. I consider God my King, against whom I've committed all sorts of crimes. Confessing my sins to Him and asking Him to forgive me, I place myself in His hands to do whatever He pleases with me.

This King, who is full of goodness and mercy, doesn't punish me. Rather, He embraces me lovingly and invites me to eat at His table. He serves me Himself and gives me the keys to His treasury, treating me as His favorite. He converses with me without mentioning either my sins or His forgiveness. My former habits are seemingly forgotten. Although I beg Him to do whatever He wishes with me, He does nothing but caress me. This is what being in His holy presence is like.

My day-to-day life consists of giving God my simple, loving attention. If I am distracted, He calls me back in tones that are supernaturally beautiful. If you think of me, remember the grace with which God has blessed me rather than my typically human ineptitude.

My prayers consist of a simple continuation of this same exercise. Sometimes I imagine that I'm a piece of stone, waiting for the sculptor. When I give myself to God this way, He begins sculpting my soul into the perfect image of His beloved Son. At other times, I feel my whole mind and heart being raised up into God's presence, as if, without effort, they had always belonged there.

Some people may consider this attitude self-deceptive. But I cannot permit it to be called deception, since in this state of enjoying God I desire nothing but His presence. If I am deceiving myself, the Lord will have to remedy it. I want Him to do whatever He pleases with me; all I want is to be completely His.

Your suggestions as to how I should handle all of this will help me, because I respect your opinion very much.

I remain yours in Christ.

Sixth Letter

*D*ear sister,

As I promised, I am praying for you, even though my prayers are meager. Wouldn't we be happy if we could find the full treasure described in the Gospel? Nothing else matters. This treasure is infinite; the more we explore it, the more riches we find. May we never stop searching until we have found all of it!

I don't know what's to become of me. It seems that a tranquil soul and a quiet spirit come to me even while I sleep. Because I am at rest, the trials of life bring me no suffering. I don't know what God has in store for me, but I feel so serene that it doesn't matter. What do I have to be afraid of when I'm with Him? I stay with Him as much as I can. May He be blessed for everything! Amen.

Seventh Letter

D *ear friend,*

We have a God who is infinitely good and who knows what He is doing. He will come and deliver you from your present trouble in His perfect time and when you may least expect it. Hope in Him more than ever. Thank Him for the strength and patience He is giving you, even in the midst of this trial, for it is an evident mark of His concern for you. Encourage yourself with His love and thank Him for everything.

I admire the strength and courage of your friend, the soldier. God has given him a fine character, even though he is still a little worldly and immature. I hope that the problems God has allowed him to have will cause him to become more concerned about his spiritual life. Encourage him to put all his confidence in God, who is always with him. He needs to communicate with God at all times, especially in the greatest dangers.

Lifting his heart up to God is sufficient. Remembering Him briefly or praising Him even in the midst of battle is very pleasing to God. And, far from destroying a soldier's courage, this will strengthen him.

Tell him to dwell in God as much as possible, gradually getting used to this simple, but holy, exercise. No one will be able to see it. Besides, nothing is easier than praising the Lord.

Tell him to do this as often as he can. It is quite acceptable behavior for a soldier; in fact, it is necessary for someone whose life (and salvation) are constantly in danger.

I pray that God will help him and all of his family, whom I salute.

Eighth Letter

$\mathcal{D}$*ear friend,*

You aren't the only one to be distracted from the presence of God; I understand completely. Our minds are so flighty. However, remember that our God-given wills govern all of our strength. We must recall our minds to God. Otherwise, our spirits may wander, dragging us down to the things of this earth.

I think the remedy for the problem is to confess our faults to God and humble ourselves before Him. It isn't necessary to be too verbose in prayer, because lengthy prayers encourage wandering thoughts. Simply present yourself to God as if you were a poor man knocking on the door of a rich man, and fix your attention on His presence. If your mind wanders at times, don't be upset, because being upset will only distract you more. Allow your will to recall your attention gently to God. Such perseverance will please Him.

Another way to prevent the mind from wandering away from God during prayer is to train yourself to dwell in His presence all day long. This will provide a sort of "practice" for you, as you remind yourself to concentrate on Him. Remaining in His presence during prayer time will thus become easier.

You know from my other letters how advantageous I think it is to practice the presence of God. Let's take this act of loving God seriously and pray for one another.

I remain your brother in Christ.

Ninth Letter

*D*ear friend,

Here is the answer to the letter I received from our dear sister in the Lord; please give it to her. She seems so full of good will, but she wants to go faster than grace allows. It is not possible to become spiritually mature all at once. I recommend that you work with her, because we should help each other with our advice and, even more, with our good example. I would appreciate your sending me news of her from time to time, so that I may know how she is coming along.

Let us often remember, my dear friend, that our sole occupation in life is to please God. What meaning can anything else have? You and I have walked with the Lord for more than forty years. Have we really used those years to love and serve God, who, by His mercy, called us for that purpose? When I consider the blessings God has given and still continues to give me, I feel ashamed. I feel I have abused those blessings, barely using them profitably to become more like Christ.

Still, God in His mercy gives us a little more time. We can begin all over again and repair the lost opportunity, returning with complete confidence to this kind Father, who is always ready to receive us lovingly. We need to abandon everything that isn't of God. Doesn't He deserve this and much more? Let's think of Him continually, and put all our confidence in Him. Soon His abundant grace will engulf us. With it, we can do anything, but without it, we can commit only sin.

We cannot avoid the dangers of life without God's continual help, so we should ask Him for it ceaselessly. But how can we ask for help unless we are with Him? To be with Him, we must cultivate the holy habit of thinking of Him often.

You will tell me that I always say the same thing. What can I say? It is true. I don't know an easier method, nor do I practice any other, so I advise this one to everybody. We have to know someone before we can truly love him. In order to know God, we must think about Him often. Once we get to know Him, we will think about Him even more often, because where our treasure is, there also is our heart!

Tenth Letter

*D*ear Madame,

It was difficult for me to decide whether or not to write to our brother in the Lord. I do so only because you wish it. Would you mind addressing and sending the letter yourself?

Your confidence in God is beautiful; may He bless you for it. We can never trust this Friend of ours too much. He is so good and so faithful never to fail us, either in this world or in the next.

I pray that our brother is wise enough to profit from his loss and to trust God completely. Perhaps our Lord will give him another friend who is more powerful and better disposed. After all, God deals with our hearts according to His will.

There may have been too much of the world in his love. He may have been too attached to the one he lost. Even though we should love our friends, that love shouldn't hinder our love of God, who must be first.

Remember what I advised you to do: Think about God as often as you can, day and night, in everything you do. He is always with you. Just as you would be rude if you deserted a friend who was visiting you, why would you be disrespectful of God by abandoning His presence?

Do not forget Him! Think of Him often. Adore Him ceaselessly. Live and die with Him. That is the real business of Christians; in a word, it is our profession. If we do not know it, we must learn it. I will pray for you.

Eleventh Letter

*D*ear friend,

Since you are so seriously interested in knowing how I attained the ability God granted me to dwell in His presence, I will try to explain it. But I must ask you not to show my letter to anyone. If I thought you were going to let someone else read it, I would not discuss the matter, despite all of my desire for your spiritual growth.

Although I found several books describing how to know God and mature spiritually, I believed they would only serve to confuse my soul. What I wanted was simply to belong totally to God, so I decided to give everything I could give in order to attain the greatest blessing in return—knowing Him. I gave myself completely to God, accepting His forgiveness of my sins, after which I renounced everything that might offend Him. I began to live as if there were no one but God and myself in the world.

Sometimes I thought of myself as a criminal standing before Him, my Judge; at other times I regarded Him as my Father. I tried to keep my heart in this father/child relationship as much as I could, adoring Him there. I held my spirit in His holy presence, recalling it whenever it went astray. This exercise was rather difficult. Yet, I was able to continue it without being disturbed when I was involuntarily distracted. It occupied as much time during my regular working day as it did in my prayer time. At all times — every hour and every minute — I drove everything out of my spirit that might take me from the thought of God.

This has been my everyday routine since I began my walk with the Lord. Although sometimes I practice it timidly and with a great many mistakes, I am still quite blessed by it. This has to be due to the great goodness and mercy of God. We can indeed do nothing without Him (which is truer for me than for others). Yet, when we faithfully keep ourselves in His holy presence and always remember that He is before us, we avoid offending Him (at least voluntarily). Then we may take the holy liberty of asking Him for the grace we need. By continuing this practice of His presence, He becomes more familiar to us, and His presence becomes a natural thing.

Thank God for His goodness to us!

Twelfth Letter

H *ello friend!*

Take courage! God often allows us to go through difficulties to purify our souls and to teach us to rely on Him more (1 Peter 1:6–7). So offer Him your problems unceasingly, and ask Him for the strength to overcome them. Talk to Him often. Forget Him as seldom as possible. Praise Him. When the difficulties are at their worst, go to Him humbly and lovingly—as a child goes to a loving father—and ask for the help you need from His grace. I will support you with my humble prayers.

God has various ways of drawing us to Him, but sometimes He hides from us. In those times, the sole support of our confidence must be our faith, which must be totally in God. Such faith will not fail.

Remember that God never leaves us unless we go away first. We should be careful never to separate ourselves from His presence. We must dwell with Him always; so let us live with Him now and die with Him when our time is at hand. Pray to Him for me, and I will for you.

I remain yours in our Lord.

Thirteenth Letter

*D*ear friend,

I cannot thank God enough for the way He has begun to deliver you from your trial.

God knows very well what we need and that all He does is for our good. If we knew how much He loves us, we would always be ready to face life—both its pleasures and its troubles.

The difficulties of life do not have to be unbearable. It is the way we look at them—through faith or unbelief—that makes them seem so. We must be convinced that our Father is full of love for us and that He only permits trials to come our way for our own good.

Let us occupy ourselves entirely in knowing God. The more we know Him, the more we will desire to know Him. As love increases with knowledge, the more we know God, the more we will truly love Him. We will learn to love Him equally in times of distress or in times of great joy.

Although we seek and love God because of the blessings He has given us or for those He may give us in the future, let's not stop there. These blessings, as great as they are, will never carry us as near to Him as a simple act of faith does in a time of need or trouble.

Let us look to God with these eyes of faith. He is within us; we don't need to seek Him elsewhere. We have only ourselves to blame if we turn from God, occupying ourselves instead with the trifles of life. In His patience, the Lord endures our weaknesses. Even so, just think of the price we pay by being separated from His presence!

Once and for all, let us begin to be His entirely. May we banish from our hearts and souls all that does not reflect Jesus. Let's ask Him for the grace to do this, so that He alone might rule in our hearts.

I must confide in you, my dear friend, that I hope, in His grace, that I will see Him in a few days.

Let's pray to Him for one another.

❖ ◈ ❖

On February 12, 1691, just a few days after writing this letter, Brother Lawrence passed from this life into the next to dwell fully in the presence of his God.

Part Three

❖ ◆ ❖

Spiritual Maxims

Spiritual Maxims

*A*ll things are possible to him who believes; still more to him who hopes; still more to him who loves; and most of all to him who practices all three. All of us who believe as we should and are baptized have taken the first step toward perfection. We will attain perfection if we practice the following principles of Christian conduct.

❖ ◈ ❖

First of all, we need to be considerate of God in everything we do and say. Our goal should be to become perfect in our adoration of Him throughout this earthly life in preparation for all eternity. We must make a firm resolution to overcome, with God's grace, all the difficulties encountered in a spiritual life.

❖ ◈ ❖

From the outset of our Christian walk, we should remember who we are and that we are unworthy of the name of Christian, except for what Christ has done for us. In cleansing us from all our impurities, God desires to humble us and often allows us to go through a number of trials or difficulties to that end.

❖ ◈ ❖

We must believe with certainty that it is both pleasing to God and good for us to sacrifice ourselves for Him. Without this complete submission of our hearts and minds to His will, He cannot work in us to make us perfect.

❖ ◈ ❖

The more we aspire to be perfect, the more dependent we are on the grace of God. We begin to need His help with every little thing and at every moment, because without it we can do nothing. The world, the flesh, and the devil wage a fierce and continuous war on our souls. If we weren't capable of humbly depending on God for assistance, our souls would be dragged down. Although this total dependence may sometimes go against our human nature, God takes great pleasure in it. Learning to do so will bring us rest.

Essential Practices for the Spiritual Life

*T*he most holy and necessary practice in our spiritual life is the presence of God. That means finding constant pleasure in His divine company, speaking humbly and lovingly with Him in all seasons, at every moment, without limiting the conversation in any way. This is especially important in times of temptation, sorrow, separation from God, and even in times of unfaithfulness and sin.

❖ ◈ ❖

We must try to converse with God in little ways while we do our work; not in memorized prayer, not trying to recite previously formed thoughts. Rather, we should purely and simply reveal our hearts as the words come to us.

❖ ◈ ❖

We must do everything with great care, avoiding impetuous actions, which are evidence of a disordered spirit. God wants us to work gently, calmly, and lovingly with Him, asking Him to accept our work. By this continual attention to

God, we will resist the devil and cause him to flee (James 4:7).

❖ ◈ ❖

Whatever we do, even if we are reading the Word or praying, we should stop for a few minutes—as often as possible—to praise God from the depths of our hearts, to enjoy Him there in secret. Since we believe that God is always with us, no matter what we may be doing, why shouldn't we stop for awhile to adore Him, to praise Him, to petition Him, to offer Him our hearts, and to thank Him?

What could please God more than for us to leave the cares of the world temporarily in order to worship Him in our spirits? These momentary retreats serve to free us from our selfishness, which can only exist in the world. In short, we cannot show our loyalty to God more than by renouncing our worldly selves as much as a thousand times a day to enjoy even a single moment with Him.

This doesn't mean we must ignore the duties of the world forever; that would be impossible. Let prudence be our guide. However, I do believe that it is a common mistake of Spirit-filled people not to leave the cares of the world periodically to praise God in their spirits and to rest in the peace of His divine presence for a few moments.

❖ ◈ ❖

Our adoration of God should be done in faith, believing that He really lives in our hearts and that He must be loved and served in spirit and in truth. We need to realize that He is the Independent One, upon whom all of us depend, and that He is aware of everything that happens to us.

The Lord's perfections are truly beyond measure. By His infinite excellence and His sovereign place as both Creator and Savior, He has the right to possess us and all that exists in both heaven and earth. It should be His good pleasure to do with each of us whatever He chooses through all time and eternity. Because of all He is to us, we owe Him our thoughts, words, and actions. Let us earnestly endeavor to do this.

❖ ◈ ❖

We must carefully examine ourselves to see which virtues we are in most need of and which we find the hardest to acquire. We should also take note of the sins that we most frequently fall into and what occasions contribute to our fall. In our times of struggle with these areas, we can go before God with entire confidence and remain in the presence of His divine majesty. In humble adoration, we must confess our sins and weaknesses to Him, lovingly asking for the help of His grace in our time of need. Then, we will find that we can partake of all the virtues found in Him, even though we do not possess any of our own.

How to Adore God

*T*o adore God in spirit and in truth means to adore Him as we should. Because God is a Spirit, He must be adored in spirit. That is to say, we must worship Him with a humble, sincere love that comes from the depth and center of our souls. Only God can see this adoration, which we must repeat until it becomes part of our nature, as if God were one with our souls and our souls were one with God. Practice will demonstrate this.

❖ ◈ ❖

Second, to adore God in truth is to recognize Him for what He is and ourselves for what we are. Adoring God in truth means that our hearts actually see God as infinitely perfect and worthy of our praise. What man, no matter how little sense he may have, would not exert all his strength to show his respect and love of this great God?

❖ ◈ ❖

Third, to adore God in truth is to admit that our nature is just the opposite of His. Yet, He is willing to make us like Him, if we desire it. Who would be so rash as to neglect, even for a moment, the respect, the love, the service, and the continual adoration that we owe Him?

The Union of the Soul with God

The first way in which the soul is united with God is through salvation, solely by His grace.

This is followed by a period in which a saved soul comes to know God through a series of experiences, some of which bring the soul into closer union with Him and some take it further away. The soul learns which activities bring God's presence nearer and remains in His presence by practicing those activities.

The most intimate union with God is the actual presence of God. Although this relationship with God is totally spiritual, it is quite dynamic, because the soul is not asleep; rather, it is powerfully excited. In this state, the soul is livelier than fire and brighter than the unclouded sun, yet, at the same time, it is tender and devout.

This union is not a simple expression of the heart, like saying, "Lord, I love You with all my heart," or other similar words. Rather, it is an inexpressible state of the soul—gentle, peaceful,

respectful, humble, loving, and very simple—
that urges the person to love God, to adore Him,
and to embrace Him with both tenderness and
joy.

Everyone who is striving for divine union
must realize that, just because something is
agreeable and delightful to the will, this does
not mean that it will bring one closer to God.
Sometimes it is helpful to disengage the sentiments of the will from the world, in order to focus entirely on God. If the will is able in some
manner to comprehend Him, this can be only by
love. And that love, which has its end in God,
will be hindered by the things of this world.

The Presence of God

*T*he presence of God is the concentration of the soul's attention on God, remembering that He is always present.

I know a person who for forty years has practiced the presence of God, to which he gives several other names. Sometimes he calls it a simple act – a clear and distinct knowledge of God – and sometimes he calls it a vague view or a general, loving look at God – a remembrance of Him. He also refers to it as attention to God, silent communion with God, confidence in God, or the life and the peace of the soul. To sum up, this person has told me that all these descriptions of the presence of God are merely synonyms that signify the same thing, a reality that has become natural to him.

My friend says that by dwelling in the presence of God he has established such a sweet communion with the Lord that His spirit abides, without much effort, in the restful peace of God. In this center of rest, he is filled with a faith that equips him to handle anything that comes into his life.

This is what he calls the "actual presence" of God, which includes any and all kinds of communion a person who still dwells on the earth can possibly have with God in heaven. At times, he can live as if no one else existed on earth but himself and God. He lovingly speaks with God wherever he goes, asking Him for all he needs and rejoicing with Him in a thousand ways.

Nevertheless, one should realize that this conversation with God occurs in the depth and center of the soul. It is there that the soul speaks to God heart to heart and always dwells in a great and profound peace that the soul enjoys in God. The trouble that happens in the world can become like a blaze of straw that goes out even as it is catching fire, while the soul retains its interior peace in God.

The presence of God is, then, the life and nourishment of the soul, which can be acquired with the grace of God. Here are the means to do so.

The Means of Acquiring God's Presence

T he first means of acquiring the presence of God is a new life, received by salvation through the blood of Christ.

❖ ◈ ❖

The second is faithfully practicing God's presence. This must always be done gently, humbly, and lovingly, without giving way to anxiety or problems.

❖ ◈ ❖

Next, the soul's eyes must be kept on God, particularly when something is being done in the outside world. Since much time and effort are needed to perfect this practice, one should not be discouraged by failure. Although the habit is difficult to form, it is a source of divine pleasure once it is learned.

It is proper that the heart—which is the first to live and which dominates all the other parts of the body—should be the first and the last to love God. The heart is the beginning and the end of all our spiritual and bodily actions and, generally speaking, of everything we do in our lives. It is, therefore, the heart whose attention we must carefully focus on God.

❖ ◈ ❖

Then, in the beginning of this practice, it would not be wrong to offer short phrases that are inspired by love, such as "Lord, I am all Yours," "God of love, I love You with all my heart," or "Lord, use me according to Your will." However, remember to keep the mind from wandering or returning to the world. Hold your attention on God alone by exercising your will to remain in His presence.

❖ ◈ ❖

Finally, although this exercise may be difficult at first to maintain, it has marvelous effects on the soul when it is faithfully practiced. It draws the graces of the Lord down in abundance and shows the soul how to see God's presence everywhere with a pure and loving vision, which is the holiest, firmest, easiest, and the most effective attitude for prayer.

The Blessings of the Presence of God

The first blessing that the soul receives from the practice of the presence of God is that its faith is livelier and more active everywhere in our lives. This is particularly true in difficult times, since it obtains the grace we need to deal with temptation and to conduct ourselves in the world. The soul—accustomed by this exercise to the practice of faith—can actually see and feel God by simply entering His presence. It envokes Him easily and obtains what it needs. In so doing, the soul could be said to approach the Blessed, in that it can almost say, "I no longer believe, but I see and experience." This faith becomes more and more penetrating as it develops through practice.

❖ ◈ ❖

Second, the practice of the presence of God strengthens us in hope. Our hope increases as our faith penetrates God's secrets through practice of our holy exercise. The soul discovers in God a beauty infinitely surpassing not only that of bodies that we see on earth, but even that of the angels. Our hope increases and grows stronger, and the amount of good that it expects to enjoy—and that in some degree it tastes—reassures and sustains it.

❖ ◈ ❖

The third blessing is that this practice causes the will to rejoice at being set apart from the world, setting it aglow with the fire of holy love. This is because the soul is always with God, who is a consuming fire, who reduces into powder whatever is opposed to Him. The soul, thus inflamed, can no longer live except in the presence of its God. This presence produces a holy ardor, a sacred urgency, and a violent desire in the heart to see this God whom the soul loves so dearly.

❖ ◈ ❖

By practicing God's presence and continuously looking at Him, the soul familiarizes itself with Him to the extent that it passes almost its whole life in continual acts of love, praise, confidence, thanksgiving, offering, and petition. Sometimes all this may merge into one single act that does not end, because the soul is always in the ceaseless exercise of God's divine presence.

Part Four

❖ ◈ ❖

The Life of
Brother Lawrence

The Life of Brother Lawrence

This account of Brother Lawrence's life was written and published shortly after his death by his dear friend, Joseph de Beaufort.

A truth that constantly recurs in Holy Scripture is that the arm of God is not shortened, since His mercy cannot be exhausted by our miseries. The power of His grace is no less great today than it was in the the first days of the church. God desired to keep saints for Himself until the end of the world. These saints would pay Him a respect worthy of His grandeur and majesty and would be models of virtue because of the holy example they set.

God was not content to have these extraordinary men born in the early centuries only. He still raises up people who perfectly fulfill these two duties of a saint and who guard the fruits of the Spirit in themselves, transmit them, and make them live again in others.

Such a man was Brother Lawrence of the Resurrection, a Carmelite lay-brother. God caused him to be born in these latter days to reverence Him and to provide an example of the faithful practice of all the virtues.

His worldly name was Nicholas Herman. His parents, upright people who led exemplary lives, taught him in his childhood to love the Lord. They were particularly careful about his education, giving him only those lessons that were consistent with the Gospel.

When he was a young man, he joined the armed services. Conducting himself with simplicity and honesty, he began to receive evidence from God of His goodness and His mercy.

To begin with, he was taken prisoner by a small body of German troops and treated as a spy. Who can imagine how far his patience and calmness went during this disagreeable event?

The Germans even threatened to hang him. He simply answered that he was not what they supposed, adding that, since he had never done anything to give him a bad conscience, death didn't frighten him anyway. When the officers in charge heard this, they released him.

Later, our young soldier was wounded, and his injury forced him to retire to the home of his parents, who were not far away. This gave him the opportunity to undertake a more holy profession—fighting under the banner of Jesus Christ. He resolved to give himself wholly to God and to repair his past conduct, not because of vanity, but through sentiments of true devotion. God then allowed him to perceive the nothingness of the pleasures of the world and touched him with a love of heavenly things.

Not realizing the fullness of God's grace, Brother Lawrence did not permit that grace to alleviate his problems immediately. He struggled with serious concerns about his profession, the corruption of the world, man's instability and infidelity, and the treason of enemies. The eternal truth of the Lord, however, finally allowed him to conquer those fears. He made a firm resolution to accept the teachings of the Gospel and walk in the footprints of Jesus Christ.

This brought a new light to his countenance. It freed him from the difficulties that the devil and the world normally put in the path of those who wish to give their lives to the Lord. Our brother acquired a prudent firmness, which gave him such a strong determination to follow God that all his former difficulties were washed away in a moment, as if by a miracle. Meditating on the promises of the Lord and his love for Jesus Christ changed him into another man. The humility of the cross became more desirable to him than all the glory the world had to offer.

Filled with a divine zeal, Brother Lawrence sought God in the simplicity and the sincerity of his heart. Because his soul was weary of the painful life he had been leading up to that time in the world, he decided to retire to the desert. There, through his new Christian strength, he was able to get closer to God than he had ever been.

However, such a solitary life is not good for young Christians, which our brother soon discovered. Seeing how joy and then sadness, peace and then anxiety, confidence and then heaviness took turns ruling his soul, Brother Lawrence began to doubt the wisdom of his decision to live in the desert, wishing instead to live within a Christian brotherhood. Life within such a group would be based on the firm rock of Jesus Christ rather than on the shifting sands of temporary, individual devotion. Also, the members of the group could edify and exhort one another, protecting themselves against the changeableness of their individual whims. Although the first step was difficult, he was lovingly persuaded by God to go to Paris, where he became a lay-brother of the Carmelite Order and took the name of Brother Lawrence.

From the very beginning, prayer was of particular importance to him. No matter how much work he had to do, he never cut his prayer time short. Recalling God's presence and the love that resulted from it soon made him the model of his fellow members in the monastery. Although he was assigned the humblest duties there, he never complained. The grace of Jesus Christ sustained him in everything that was unpleasant or tiresome.

His faithfulness to God was exemplary. Even when mistakenly told by one of his superiors that there was talk of dismissing him from the monastery, he replied, "I am in the hands of God; He will do with me as He pleases. If I do not serve Him here, I will serve Him elsewhere."

However, as Brother Lawrence attempted to move into a more spiritual life, memories of the sins of his past life engulfed him, and he judged himself a great sinner, unworthy of any of God's attentions. This led to ten years of intense fear and anxiety in which he often doubted his salvation. With an afflicted heart, he would pour out his troubles to God. But his own fears of what it would cost to serve God completely caused him to resist God's total salvation.

In this bitter, dark time, Brother Lawrence found little comfort in prayer, but nevertheless he continued to pray. Placing his trust in God, his uppermost desire was still to please Him.

Even when he felt he should give it up completely, he found the inner strength and courage to endure. Finally, he cried out to God, "It no longer matters to me what I do or what I suffer, as long as I remain lovingly united to Your will."

This is precisely the disposition God wanted him to develop before pouring out the blessings of His presence. What our humble brother had not known was just how merciful God is toward sinners such as himself. He didn't realize he had already been forgiven. However, from then on, the firmness of his soul grew greater than ever. God, who can accomplish wondrous things in a moment, suddenly opened Brother Lawrence's eyes. He received a divine revelation of God's majesty that illuminated his spirit, dissipated all his fears, and ended his inner struggles and pain. From that moment, meditating on the character and lovingkindness of God molded Brother Lawrence's character. It became so natural to him that he passed the last forty years of his life in continuous practice of the presence of God, which he described as a quiet, familiar conversation with Him.

Brother Lawrence began this practice by cultivating a deep presence of God in his heart. He said that God's presence had to be maintained by the heart and by love rather than by understanding and speech.

"In the way of God," he said, "thoughts count for little, love does everything. And it is not necessary to have great things to do. I turn my little omelet in the pan for the love of God; when it is finished, if I have nothing to do, I prostrate myself on the ground and adore my God, who gave me the grace to make it, after which I arise, more content than a king. When I cannot do anything else, it is enough for me to have lifted a straw from the earth for the love of God.

"People seek for methods of learning to love God. They hope to arrive at it by I know not how many different practices; they take much trouble to remain in the presence of God in a quantity of ways. Is it not much shorter and more direct to do everything for the love of God, to make use of all the labors of one's state in life to show Him that love, and to maintain His presence within us by this communion of our hearts with His? There is no finesse about it; one has only to do it generously and simply."

When one of the brothers persistently questioned Brother Lawrence about his means of practicing the presence of God, he answered with his usual simplicity:

"When I first entered the monastery, I looked upon God as the beginning and the end of all my thoughts and all the feelings of my soul. During the hours that were designated for prayer, I meditated on the truth and character of God that we must accept by the light of faith, rather than spending time in laborious meditations and readings. By meditating on Jesus

Himself, I advanced in my knowledge of this lovable Person with whom I resolved to dwell always.

"Completely immersed in my understanding of God's majesty, I used to shut myself up in the kitchen. Alone, after having done everything that was necessary for my work, I devoted myself to prayer in the time that was left.

"The prayer time was really taken at both the beginning and the end of my work. At the beginning of my duties, I would say to the Lord with confidence, 'My God, since You are with me and since, by Your will, I must occupy myself with external things, please grant me the grace to remain with You, in Your presence. Work with me, so that my work might be the very best. Receive as an offering of love both my work and all my affections.'

"During my work, I would always continue to speak to the Lord as though He were right with me, offering Him my services and thanking Him for His assistance. Also, at the end of my work, I used to examine it carefully. If I found good in it, I thanked God. If I noticed faults, I asked His forgiveness without being discouraged, and then went on with my work, still dwelling in Him.

"Thus, continuing in the practice of conversing with God throughout each day and quickly seeking His forgiveness when I fell or strayed, His presence has become as easy and natural to me now as it once was difficult to attain."

After Brother Lawrence began to realize the great blessings this holy experience brings to the soul, he advised all of his friends to practice it as carefully and faithfully as they could. Wanting them to undertake this act with a firm resolution and courage, he used the strongest reasons he could to persuade them. In his spiritual enthusiasm and by his godly example, he not only touched their minds, but also penetrated their very hearts. He helped them to love and undertake this holy practice with as much fervor as they had previously regarded it with indifference. His example truly did serve better than his words. One had only to look at Brother Lawrence to desire to dwell in God's presence even as he did, no matter how rushed one might be.

Brother Lawrence called the practice of the presence of God the easiest and shortest way to attain Christian perfection and to be protected from sin.

Even when he was busiest in the kitchen, it was evident that the brother's spirit was dwelling in God. He often did the work that two usually did, but he never seemed to bustle. Rather, he gave each chore the time that it required, always preserving his modest and tranquil air, working neither slowly nor swiftly, dwelling in calmness of soul and unalterable peace.

In this intimate union with the Lord, our brother's passions grew so calm that he scarcely felt them any more. He developed a gentle disposition, complete honesty, and the most charitable heart in the world. His kind face, his gracious and affable air, his simple and modest manner immediately won him the esteem and the good will of everyone who saw him. The more familiar with him they became, the more they became aware of how profoundly upright and reverent he was.

Despite his simple and common life in the monastery, he did not pretend to be austere or melancholy, which only serves to rebuff people. On the contrary, he fraternized with everyone and treated his brothers as friends, without trying to be distinguished from them. He never took the graces of God for granted and never paraded his virtues in order to win esteem, trying rather to lead a hidden and unknown life. Though he was indeed a humble man, he never sought the glory of humility, but only its reality. He wanted no one but God to witness what he did, just as the only reward he expected was God Himself.

Although he was by nature reserved, he had no difficulty communicating his thoughts for the edification of his brothers. It was observed, however, that he favored those who were simpler and less sophisticated in their walk with Christ over the more enlightened. When he found such Christians, he shared everything he knew with them. With wonderful simplicity, Brother Lawrence disclosed to them the fairest secrets of the spiritual life and the treasures of divine wisdom. The sweetness that accompanied his words so inspired those who listened that they came away penetrated with the love of God, burning with the desire to put the great truths he had just taught them into practice.

Because God led Brother Lawrence more by love than by the fear of His judgment, his conversation tended to inspire the same kind of love. He encouraged other Christians to rely on God's love to lead them in their spiritual lives, rather than the knowledge of learned men. He used to tell his brothers, "It is the Creator who teaches truth, who in one moment instructs the heart of the humble and makes him understand more about the mysteries of our faith and even about Himself than if he had studied them for a long term of years."

It was for this reason that he carefully avoided answering those curious questions that lead nowhere and that serve only to burden the spirit and dry up the heart. However, when he was required by his superiors to declare his thoughts on the difficult questions that were proposed in conferences, his answers were always so clear and to the point that they needed no further comment. This remarkable ability was noticed by many learned men. An illustrious bishop of France, who had had several interviews with him, said that God spoke directly to Brother Lawrence, revealing His divine mysteries to him because of the greatness and the purity of his love for Him.

Brother Lawrence loved to seek God in the things He had created. His soul, moved by the grandeur and the diversity of God's creations, became so powerfully attached to God that nothing could separate it from Him. He observed in each of creation's wonders God's wisdom, His goodness, and the different characteristics of His power. His spirit would become so filled at these times with admiration that he would cry out in love and joy, "O Lord God, how incomprehensible You are in Your thoughts, how profound in Your designs, how powerful in all Your actions."

Brother Lawrence's Christian walk began with this profound understanding of the power and the wisdom of God. This knowledge became the seed of all his excellence. In the beginning, faith was the only light he used to get to know

God. As he matured, he would let nothing but faith guide him in all of God's ways. He often said that everything he heard, everything he found written in books, and even everything that he himself wrote seemed pale in comparison to what faith revealed to him of the glory of God the Father and of Jesus Christ. He expressed this to me in these words:

"God alone is capable of making Himself known as He really is; we search in reasoning and in the sciences, as in a poor copy, for what we neglect to see in an excellent original. God Himself paints Himself in the depths of our souls. We must enliven our faith and elevate ourselves by means of that faith, above all our feelings, to adore God the Father and Jesus Christ in all their divine perfections. This way of faith is the mind of the church, and it suffices to arrive at high perfection."

Brother Lawrence's principal virtue was his faith. As the just man lives by faith, so it was the life and nourishment of his soul. His spiritual life progressed visibly because of the way his faith quickened his soul. This great faith led him to God, elevating him above the world, which came to appear contemptible in his eyes. As a result, he sought happiness in God alone.

Faith was his greatest instructor. It was faith that gave him an unspeakably high esteem for

Jesus Christ, the Son of God who resides as King. He was so devoted to Jesus that he passed many hours, day and night, at His feet to render Him homage and adoration.

This same faith gave him a profound respect and love for the Word of God. Our brother believed that the books of even the most famous academies taught very little in comparison with God's great Book. With such conviction did he believe the faith-taught truth that he often used to say nothing he could read or hear in the world about God could satisfy him. Lawrence declared, "Because God's perfection is infinite, He is consequently indescribable; no words of man are eloquent enough to give a complete description of His grandeur. It is only faith that makes me know Him as He is. By means of it, I learn more about Him in a short time than I would learn in many years in the schools."

Faith gave Brother Lawrence a firm hope in God's goodness, confidence in His providence, and the ability to completely abandon himself into God's hands. He never worried about what would become of him; rather, he threw himself into the arms of infinite mercy. The more desperate things appeared to him, the more he hoped—like a rock beaten by the waves of the sea and yet settling itself more firmly in the midst of the tempest. This is why he said that the greatest glory one can give to God is to entirely mistrust one's own strength, relying completely on God's protection. This constitutes a sincere recognition of one's weakness and a true confession of the omnipotence of the Creator.

Brother Lawrence saw nothing but the plan of God in everything that happened to him. Because he loved the will of the Lord so much, he was able to bring his own will into complete submission to it. This kept him in continuous peace. Even when told of some great evil in the world, He would simply raise his heart to God, trusting that He would work it to the good of the general order. Even when asked what he would answer if God gave him the choice of living or dying and going to heaven immediately, Brother Lawrence said that he would leave the choice to God because he had nothing else to do but wait until God showed him His will.

The natural attachment to one's country that people carry with them into even the holiest places did not preoccupy him. He was equally loved by those who had different inclinations. He wished for good in general, without regard to the people by whom or for whom it was done. He was a citizen of heaven, not concerned with things on earth. His views were not limited by time, because he contemplated nothing but the Eternal One and had become eternal like Him.

The love of God reigned so completely in Brother Lawrence's heart that he turned all his affections toward this divine Beloved. Faith made him regard God as sovereign truth; hope made him think of Him as complete happiness; and love caused him to conceive of Him as the most perfect of all beings, as Perfection itself.

Everything was the same to him — every place, every job. The good brother found God everywhere, as much while he was repairing shoes as while he was praying with the community. He was in no hurry to go on retreats because he found the same God to love and adore in his ordinary work as in the depth of the desert.

Brother Lawrence's only means of going to God was to do everything for the love of Him. He was thus indifferent about what he did. All that mattered was that he did it for God. It was He, and not the activity, that he considered. He knew that the more the thing he did was opposed to his natural inclination, the greater was the merit of his love in offering it to God. He knew that the pettiness of the deed would not diminish the worth of his offering, because God — needing nothing — considers in our works only the love that accompanies them.

Another characteristic of Brother Lawrence was an extraordinary firmness, which in another walk of life would have been called fearlessness. It revealed a magnanimous soul, elevated above the fear and the hope of all that was not God. He coveted nothing; nothing astonished him; he feared nothing. This stability of his soul came from the same source as all his other virtues. He had an exalted concept of God that made him think of Him as sovereign Justice and infinite Goodness. He was confident that God would not deceive him and that He would do him only good, because he was resolved never to displease Him and to do everything possible out of love for Him.

Far from loving God in return for His benefits, he would have loved Him even if there had been no punishment to avoid or any reward to gain. He desired only the glory of God and the accomplishment of His holy will. This was especially evident in his final illness, in which, even to his last breath, his spirit was so free that he expressed the same sentiments, as if he had been in perfect health.

The purity of his love was so great that he wished, if it were possible, that God could not see what he did in His service. This was so that he might act solely for God's glory and without self-interest. However, God would let nothing pass without rewarding our brother a hundred-fold, often causing him to feel delights and sensations of His divinity that were overwhelming. Then, he would cry out to God: "It is too much, O Lord! It is too much for me.

"If it please You, give these kinds of favors and consolations to sinners and to the people who don't know You, in order to attract them to Your service. As for me, who has the happiness of knowing You by faith, I think that must be sufficient. Still, because I should not refuse anything from a hand so rich and generous as Yours, I accept, O my God, the favors You give me. Yet grant, if it please You, that after having received them, I may return them just as You gave them to me; for You well know that it is not Your gifts that I seek and desire, but Yourself, and I can be content with nothing less."

These times of prayer would inflame his heart all the more with love, the effects of which he was not always able to contain. He was often seen, against his will, with his countenance quite radiant.

Regretting the early years before he dwelt in the love of God, Brother Lawrence would speak of this to his fellow brothers: "O Goodness, so ancient and so new, too late have I loved You!

"Do not act this way, my brothers. You are young; profit by the sincere confession I make to you of the little care I took to consecrate my first years to God. Consecrate all of your years to His love; for, as for me, if I had known sooner, and if anyone had told me the things that I am telling you now, I would not have waited so long to love Him. Believe me, and count for lost all the time that is not spent in loving God."

Since loving God and loving one's neighbor are really the same thing, Brother Lawrence regarded those around him with the same affection he felt for the Lord. He believed that this was what Christ expressed in the Gospel: that anything he did for even the humblest of his brothers would be counted as being done for Jesus. He was particularly careful to serve his brothers no matter what he was doing, and especially when he was working in the kitchen. There he treated them as if they were angels, a charity that he inspired in all those who succeeded him.

He assisted the poor in their needs as much as was in his power. He consoled them when they had problems, offering them his advice. To sum this up in a few words, he did all the good he could for his neighbor and tried never to harm anyone. He did everything he possibly could to win men to God.

Death did not frighten Brother Lawrence at all. On his deathbed, he displayed marks of a stability, a resignation, and a joy that were quite extraordinary. His hope became firmer and his love more ardent. If he had loved God deeply during his life, he did not love Him any less at death. The virtue he esteemed above all others — faith — became particularly vigorous, penetrating him with its grandeur and enlightening him by its radiance.

He was given some final time alone to reflect on the great grace that God had given him during his life. When asked how he spent that time, he replied that he had been doing what he would be doing for all eternity: "Blessing God, praising God, adoring Him, and loving Him with all my heart. That is our whole purpose, brothers, to adore God and to love Him, without worrying about the rest."

The next day, February 12, 1691, without any agony and without the loss of any of his senses, Brother Lawrence of the Resurrection died in the embrace of the Lord. At eighty years old, he gave back his soul to God with the peace and tranquility of a person falling asleep. His death was like a gentle slumber that helped him pass from this life into a more blessed one.

It is easy to conclude that the death of Brother Lawrence was precious in the sight of the Lord, that it was very quickly followed by his reward, and that he is now enjoying glory.

Further, we know that his faith has been rewarded by clear vision, his hopes by possession, and his budding charity by a consummate love.